igloo

This edition published in 2010
by Igloo Books Ltd
Cottage Farm, Sywell
Northants, NN6 0BJ
www.igloo-books.com

10 9 8 7
ISBN: 978-1-84561-262-7

Cover and contents illustrations by Martin Impey
Text by Rebecca Gee

Printed and manufactured in China

My Baby Record Book

My name is ....

And I was born on ....

My parents before I was born

My Mother's name is ....
Her age when she was expecting me was ....

My Father's name is ....
His age when he was expecting me was ....

This is how my parents met ....

Family tree

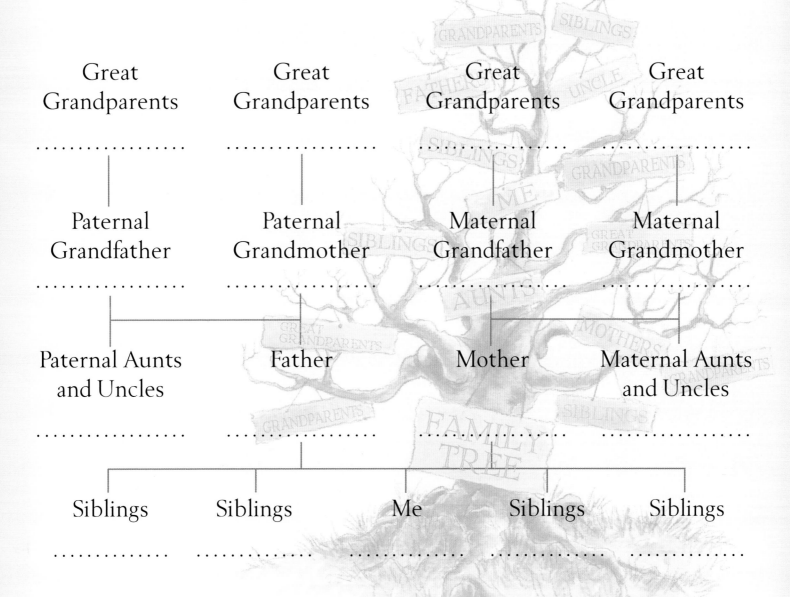

| Great Grandparents | Great Grandparents | Great Grandparents | Great Grandparents |

| Paternal Grandfather | Paternal Grandmother | Maternal Grandfather | Maternal Grandmother |

| Paternal Aunts and Uncles | Father | Mother | Maternal Aunts and Uncles |

| Siblings | Siblings | Me | Siblings | Siblings |

Waiting for me

My Mother's feelings when she found out I was on the way

. . . .

My Father's feelings when he found out I was on the way

. . . .

The foods my Mother craved were

. . . .

I was due on . . . .

This is my first baby scan picture

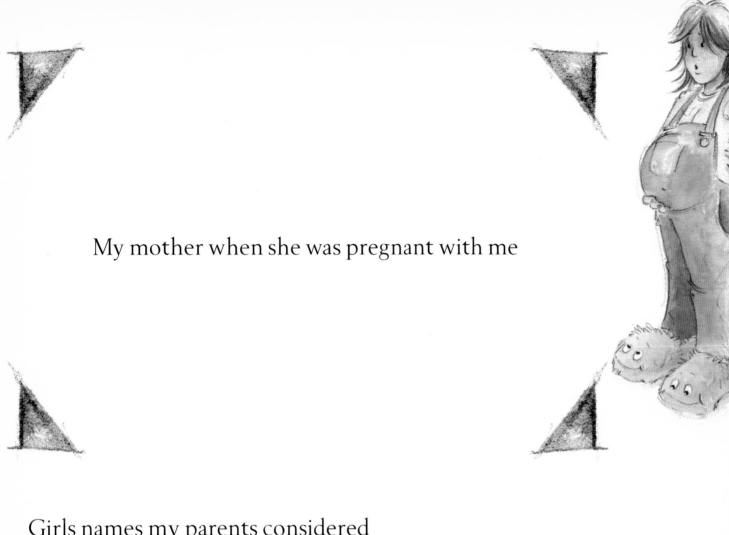

My mother when she was pregnant with me

Girls names my parents considered

....

Boys names my parents considered

....

My parents' feelings just before my birth

....

....

Here I am!

I was born at (time)

. . . .

The place I was born was

. . . .

My eye colour was . . . .

I look like . . . .   My hair was . . . .

My weight was

. . . .

My length was

. . . .

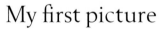

My first picture

6

Here is my hospital bracelet

My birth lasted ....

The midwife's name was ....

My name was chosen because ....

My parents' comments about the birth

....

....

My parents' first impressions of me

....

....

7

The world when I was born

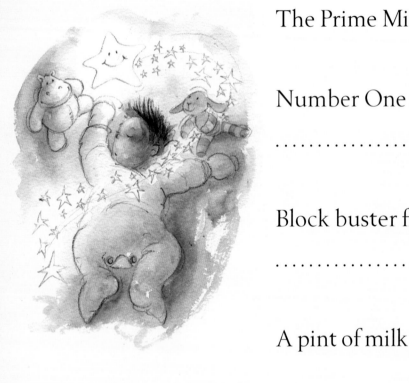

The Prime Minister was ....

Number One in the Charts was

....

Block buster films were

....

A pint of milk costs ....

A newspaper costs .... My first nappies cost ....

Fashions of the day were ....

....

....

Famous people who share
my birthday are

....

....

Historical events that happened

on my birthday are ....

....

Here are some newspaper clippings from the day I was born

Welcome home

I came home on ....

Who brought me home

....

Who was waiting for me at home

....

My address is ....

....

....

The first thing I did when I got

home was ....

The first thing my parents did when they got home was

....

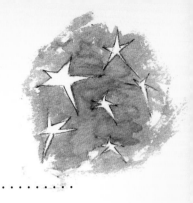

On my first night I went to sleep at

....

And woke up at

....

How I fed in the first week ....

....

How I slept in the first week ....

....

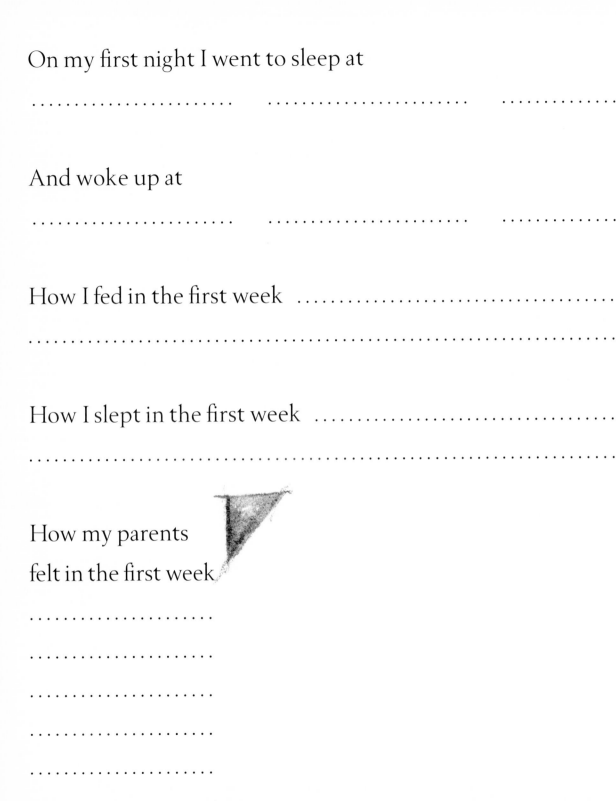

How my parents
felt in the first week

....

....

....

....

....

11

My visitors and presents

Here is a list of all my visitors and presents in the first few weeks

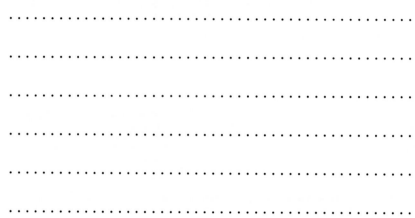

....
....
....
....
....
....
....

My hand and footprints

My hand and footprint at .... weeks

Early outings

For my first trip out I went to

....

The date was ....

This is how long it took to get me ready

....

Who took me ....

My reaction was ....

Here is a picture of me on my first outing

My pram looked like ....

My pram was given to me by ....

My first car journey was on .... with ....

What I think of the car ....

My first train trip was on .... with ....

This is what happened ....

I first went on a bus on .... with ....

This is what happened ....

A picture of me on the move

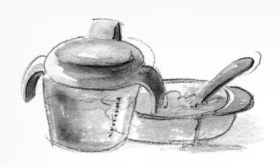

Yum, yum

The first time I ate solid foods was ....

What I ate ....

Who fed it to me ....

What I thought of it ....

I first tried finger foods ....

I first fed myself ....

I first used a beaker ....

I first sat in a highchair ....

My favourite foods are

....

....

And I particularly hate ....

....

Here is my messiest picture

17

Playtime

The person who makes me laugh the most is ....

Because ....

....

My best friend is ....

....

Age ....

We met because ....

....

Here's what we think of each other

....

Some of the things we've done together are ....

....

Here's a picture of us together

The first time I went to the playground was on ....

What I thought of it ....

My favourite game is ....

My favourite toys are ....

The strangest thing I like playing with is ....

Look what I can do!

	DATE	AGE
I first lifted my head whilst lying on my tummy	....	....
I first smiled	....	....
I first laughed	....	....
I first reached for a toy	....	....
I first rolled from my tummy to back	....	....
I first sat with support	....	....
I first sat without support	....	....
I first passed an object from one hand to another	....	....
I first clapped my hands	....	....

	DATE	AGE
I first crawled	....	....
I first started understanding words	....	....
My first word was	....	
I first pulled myself up	....	....
I first walked with a pushalong toy	....	....
I first walked alone	....	....

Splash!

I was given my first bath on .... by ....

My reaction ....

I first went in the big bath ....

My favourite bath games were ....
....

What I think of having my hair washed ....

The first time I went in a paddling pool was ....

Where it was ....

Here's what I thought of it ....

I first went swimming on .... with ....

My reaction ....

How long I slept for afterwards! ....

Bedtime

My bedtime routine ....

....

My favourite place to sleep is ....

I can't sleep without

....

....

....

....

My favourite lullabies

....

....

....

....

....

I first slept in a cot ....

I first slept through the night ....

I first slept in a bed ....

This is how I slept ....

25

My first celebrations

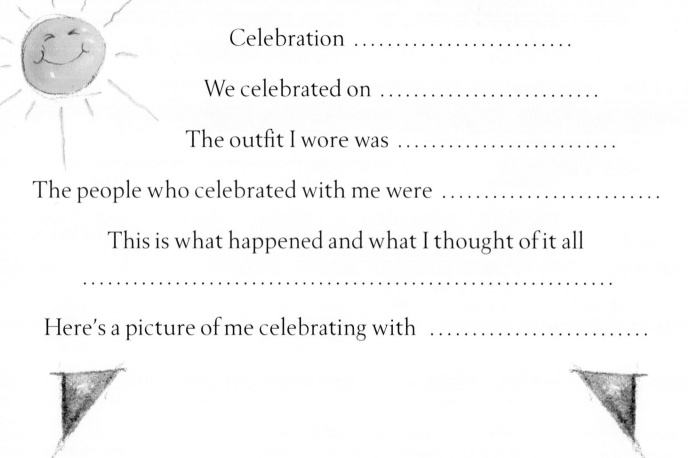

Celebration ....

We celebrated on ....

The outfit I wore was ....

The people who celebrated with me were ....

This is what happened and what I thought of it all

....

Here's a picture of me celebrating with ....

Celebration ....

We celebrated on ....

The outfit I wore was ....

The people who celebrated with me were

....

This is what happened and what I thought of it all

....

Here's a picture of me celebrating with ....

My first Christmas

My age was ....

Where I spent my first Christmas ....

Who I spent it with

....

My Christmas outfit was

....

For my first
Christmas dinner I ate

....

The Number One Song at Christmas

was ....

The weather was ....

A list of some of my presents

....

....

....

....

What I thought of the day ....

....

My first holiday

The date of my first holiday was ....

Where I went ....

Who came with me ....

How we got there ....

Here is a picture of me on holiday
with ....

What I thought of the journey ....

This is how I slept on holiday ....

What the weather was like ....

The things I liked eating on holiday were

....

The thing I hated most
about my holiday was

....

....

Here are some of the things
I did on holiday

....

....

....

....

31

My health

My health visitor's name ....

My doctor's name ....

What happened at my first review at 6−8 weeks ....

What happened at my second review at 6−9 months ....

The immunisations I received ....

This is how I reacted to my immunisations ....

My first illness was when I was .... The illness was ....

This is how I coped when I was ill ....

This is how my parents coped when I was ill! ....

My Teeth

The person who found my first tooth was

....

How I slept when I was teething

....

Other reactions when I was teething ....

First tooth appeared ....

2nd.........	8th.........	14th.........
3rd.........	9th.........	15th.........
4th.........	10th.........	16th.........
5th.........	11th.........	17th.........
6th.........	12th.........	18th.........
7th.........	13th.........	19th.........

Last tooth appeared ....

Other favourites and firsts

My favourite people are ....

What I like doing with them ....

My favourite first words were ....

....

My favourite nursery rhymes are ....

I had my first haircut on ....

The hairdresser's name was ....

This is how I reacted ....

I got my first pair of shoes on ....

This is how I reacted ....

Here is a lock of hair from my first haircut

The first time my parents went out without me was ....

They went to ....

They stayed out for ....

My babysitter was ....

This is how I behaved ....

As I grow

A picture of me at 3 months old

Weight .... Length .... Eye colour .... Hair ....

How I was feeding .... How I was sleeping ....

The best things I've learned to do ....

....

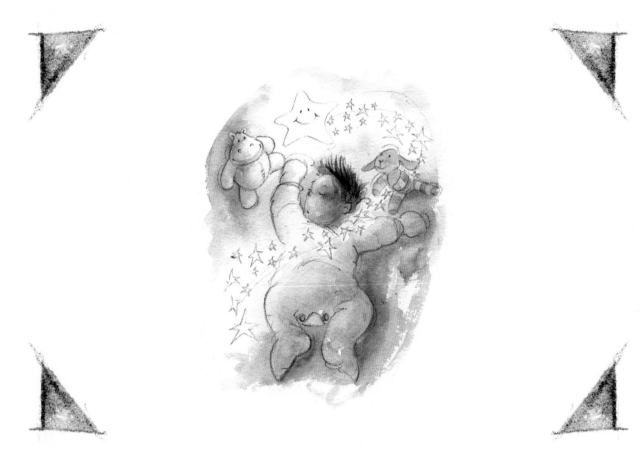

A picture of me at 6 months old

Weight .... Length .... Eye colour .... Hair ....

How I was feeding .... How I was sleeping ....

The best things I've learned to do ....

....

A picture of me at 9 months old

Weight .... Length .... Eye colour .... Hair ....

How I was feeding .... How I was sleeping ....

The best things I've learned to do ....

....

A picture of me at 12 months old

Weight .... Length .... Eye colour .... Hair ....

How I was feeding .... How I was sleeping ....

The best things I've learned to do ....

....

My first birthday

Who I celebrated with ....

What we did on the day ....

My first birthday cake was ....

Some of the presents I received ....

....

My parents' feelings about my first year

....
....
....
....

Plans for the future ....

What my parents think I will be when I grow up

....
....
....

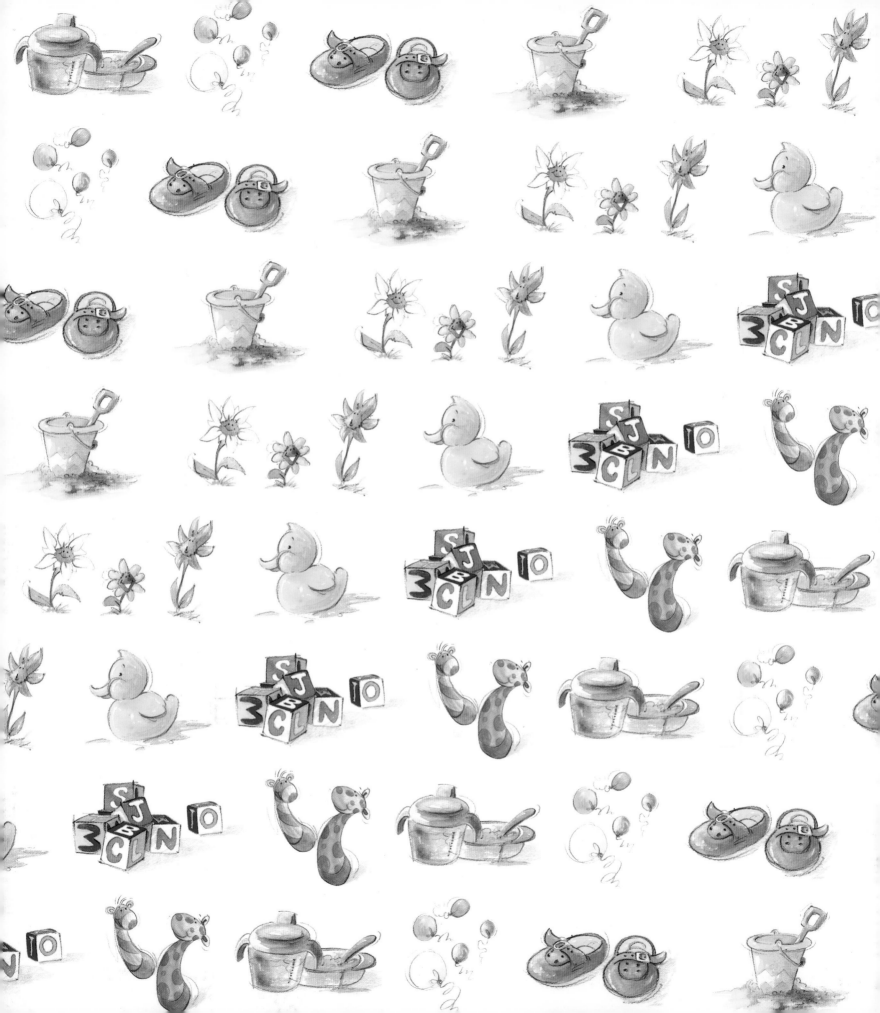